Painting
on
Rocks

for Kids

NORTH LIGHT BOOKS
CINCINNATI, OHIO
www.artistsnetwork.com

Lin Wellford

W9-CBB-876

For Skye, Erika and Kira

Painting on Rocks for Kids. © 2002 by Lin Wellford. Manufactured in China. All rights reserved. No part of this book may be reproduced in any form or by any electronic or mechanical means including information storage and retrieval systems without permission in writing from the publisher, except by a reviewer, who may quote brief passages in a review. Published by North Light Books, an imprint of F&W Publications, Inc., 4700 East Galbraith Road, Cincinnati, OH 45236. (800) 289-0963. First edition.

Other fine North Light Books are available from your local bookstore or art supply store or direct from the publisher.

06 05 04 03 02   5 4 3 2 1

Library of Congress Cataloging-in-Publication Data

Wellford, Lin
   Painting on rocks for kids / Lin Wellford.
       p. cm.
   Summary: Provides instructions for making cars, flowers, dinosaurs, food, and more from painted rocks.
   ISBN 1-58180-255-2 (alk. paper)
   1. Stone painting--Juvenile literature. 2. Acrylic painting--Juvenile literature. [1. Stone painting. 2. Handicraft.] I. Title.

TT370 . W6523 2002
745.7'23--dc21
Editor: Maggie Moschell
Cover Designer: Andrea Short
Interior Designer: Brian Roeth
Production Coordinator: Mark Griffin
Production Artist: Kathy Bergstrom
Photographers: Lin Wellford and
       Christine Polomsky

About the Author

The author at age 10

Do you know the fairy tale about the person who learns to spin straw into gold? That's what it feels like to turn plain old rocks into art! When I was younger, I liked to draw and practiced so much that I became pretty good at it, but the first time I painted a rock, I knew that I had found something really special. It feels almost like magic to take a rock and change it into a little house, a bunch of flowers or a cuddly teddy bear.

I have always loved writing, so I am very happy to have found a career that allows me to do my two most favorite things.

As you try painting your own rocks, I hope you'll remember that part of the fun is seeing how much better your results will be with time and effort. Every rock can be a "stepping stone" that takes you farther along the path to becoming an artist yourself! So, keep rockin'!

Acknowledgments

Special thanks to Erin Robertson for helping to paint many of these projects as well as providing lots of inspiration and advice. Erin is proof that you can be a real artist at any age!

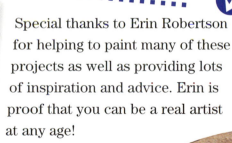

here are the projects **you can do!**

PROJECT
1
Go Fish!

PROJECT
2
Rocky Roadsters

PROJECT
3
Lazy Lizards

PROJECT
4
Flower Power

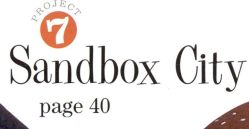

tips
for painting rocks

Rocks are a great natural art material. They come in many different shapes and sizes. By adding details with paint, you can turn rocks into all kinds of amazing things. Pick up a rock and ask yourself what it looks like.

Not all rocks are good for painting. Some are too bumpy or rough, or they soak up paint like a sponge. Look for rocks that are smooth. Rocks that have been tumbled in water, such as in a river or creek, are the easiest to paint, but you can also use chunky rocks and pieces of fieldstone as long as the sides are not too rough. You can even paint pieces of broken concrete.

◐ Always scrub your rocks before you begin painting. Paint won't stick to a dirty rock.

◐ You'll need a paper plate, plastic lid or plastic artist's palette for mixing your paint.

◐ Never let paint dry on your brushes. It turns them all stiff and yucky.

◐ Always rinse your brush between colors. Have paper towels handy for wiping your brush.

◐ Pour paint in little puddles, about the size of your thumbnail. Big puddles dry up before you can use them.

◐ Wear old clothes and push up your sleeves when you paint. If you get acrylic paint on your clothes, scrub it off with an old toothbrush, soap and plenty of water before it dries. Dried acrylic paint may never come out of fabric.

◐ Spread newspaper over your work area. You can wipe your brush and make test strokes on it. Also it will slow down a spill if you tip over your water.

And the most important thing to remember is ↴

◐ You can't ruin a rock! If you make a mistake, just wipe off the paint before it dries, or let it dry and then paint over it.

A clean paintbrush

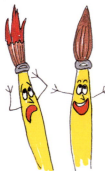

is a happy paintbrush.

Remember to rinse your brush

after each color.

Paint

tempera paint

For the projects in this book, you'll need a set of basic colors of acrylic paint. You can also decorate rocks with tempera paint, watercolors, paint pens, markers, gel pens, colored pencils or nail polish.

acrylic paint

If your painted rocks will be just for decoration indoors, the kind of paint you use doesn't matter. If your rocks are going to be used outside or soaked in water, you should use outdoor acrylic paint, which is found at most craft stores. It stays on the rocks better than regular acrylic paint.

Paintbrushes

outdoor acrylic paint

You will need just three brushes:
- a wide flat brush like the two brushes on the far right
- a medium brush like the two in the middle
- a small, skinny brush like the green one

Other helpful things
- Cotton swabs for blending
- Pencil, marker or white pencil for drawing the designs on the rocks
- Air-dry clay for rocks that tip over
- Dimensional paint for puffy lines or dots
- Acrylic floor wax for making the rocks shiny

watercolors

markers

colored pencils

brushes, paint and more

all about rocks

Where to find rocks

You may find good rocks near creeks, streams, beaches and lakes. In some areas rocks seem to be lying around everywhere, and in other places it may take a lot of hunting to find them. Don't take rocks out of the water in places where they may be homes for crayfish or other animals. State and national parks do not allow visitors to take anything home, including rocks. It's a good idea to ask for permission before you gather rocks outside your own yard.

You can buy rocks of all sizes from landscaping companies or gardening stores. Once you start looking for rocks, you'll be amazed at the unexpected places you'll find them.

Small rocks are fun, too!

Most of the rocks in this book fit into the palm of your hand. If you can't find many rocks this size, don't worry; there are still lots of things you can do with smaller rocks. Here are just a few ideas.

Make Faces
Use flat pebbles to create silly face rocks.

Put 'em Together
Use white glue and pebbles or gravel to make pictures, names or designs. Colored aquarium gravel is sold at pet stores. Make sure to allow plenty of drying time when you glue rocks.

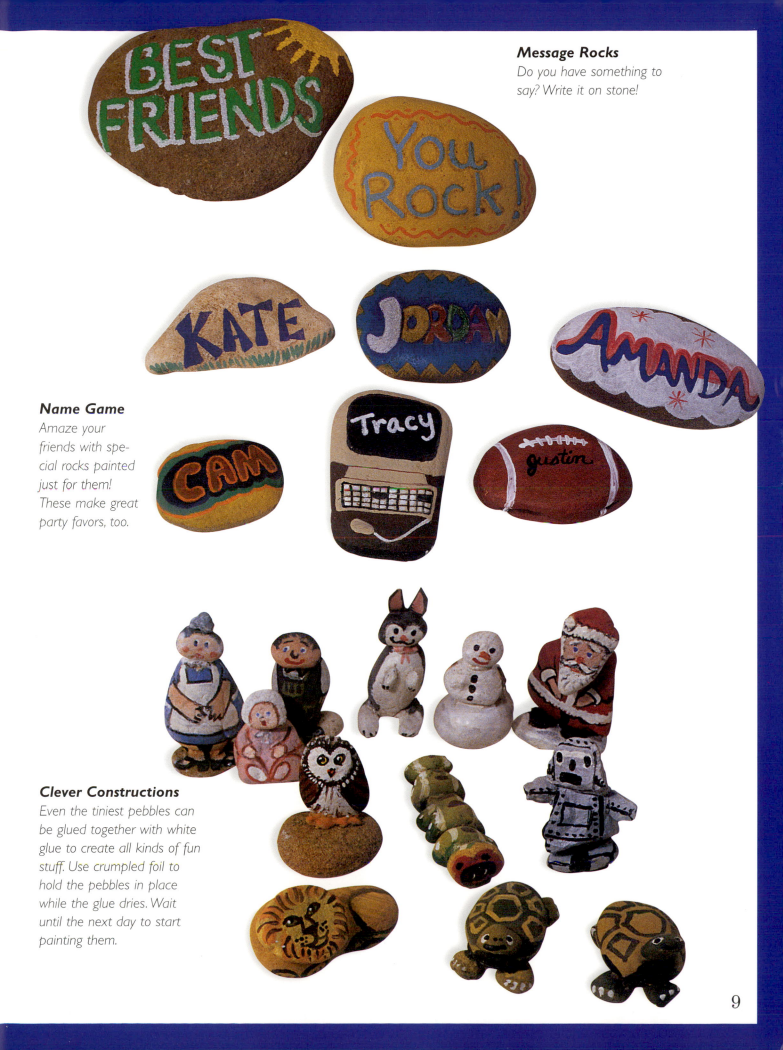

Name Game

Amaze your friends with special rocks painted just for them! These make great party favors, too.

Clever Constructions

Even the tiniest pebbles can be glued together with white glue to create all kinds of fun stuff. Use crumpled foil to hold the pebbles in place while the glue dries. Wait until the next day to start painting them.

9

go fish!

> I wanted a pet fish, but Mom said I had to wait until I was old enough to remember to feed it. At the creek I saw a rock that gave me an idea. Why not make a rock fish? A rock fish doesn't mind if I never feed him! Here's how I made mine.

Make a Fishbowl
Put gravel or marbles in the bottom of a fishbowl and add water, a plastic plant and your painted fish (painted with outdoor acrylic paint). Prop up your fish with a smaller rock. Paint other rocks to add to the scene.

What You'll Need

Rock

Pencil

Palette or paper plate

Paint of your choice*

Paintbrushes

Black marker (optional)

Glitter paint or white glue and glitter** (optional)

*If you aren't planning to put your fish in a bowl of water, you can use any kind of paint. If you are, use outdoor acrylic paint.

**White glue and glitter isn't waterproof.

Find a fish-shaped rock

Choose a smooth, flat rock that has a "fishy" shape. Pictures of real fish can give you ideas. When you find a rock you like, scrub it clean.

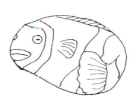
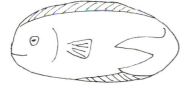
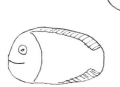
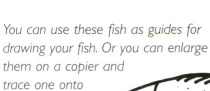

Draw the fish

Use a pencil to draw the head with a curved line and give the fish a round eye. At the other end, draw a fan-shaped tail and draw triangles above and below the tail.

You can use these fish as guides for drawing your fish. Or you can enlarge them on a copier and trace one onto your rock with carbon paper.

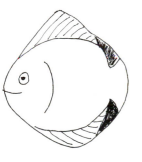

3 Paint the head

Use a bright color and your large brush to paint the fish's head. Paint all the way around the edges so no plain rock shows, but leave the circle for the eye unpainted.

4 Paint around the tail

Use black paint and your medium brush to fill in the triangles above and below the tail. The black paint makes those parts seem to disappear.

5 Outline the eye

Make a black outline around the eye with a black marker or your skinny brush, keeping the outside edge round and neat. The inside edge will get covered up later.

Remember to rinse your brush

after each color.

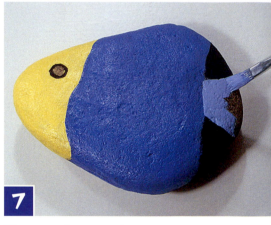

6 Paint the body

Pick a color for the body. Mix three drops of this color with one drop of white, and paint the fish's body.

7 Paint the tail

Mix three drops of white and one drop of the body color for the tail. Save this puddle of paint for step 9.

TIPS FOR PAINTING GOOD LINES

1. Thin the paint with a little water.
2. Hold your brush handle straight up.
3. Paint with just the tip of the brush.
4. Paint lines with one smooth stroke, not a lot of little sketchy lines.
5. If you mess up, wipe the line off with a damp paper towel and try again.
6. The more you practice, the better you'll get!

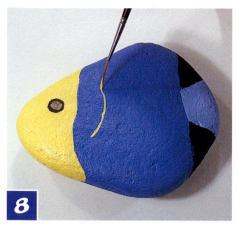

Paint the gill

When the paint on the body is dry, use your skinny brush to add a light-colored curved gill line just behind the head. I used yellow.

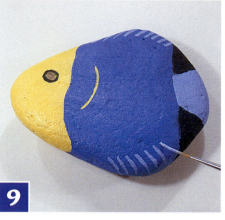

Paint fins

Clean the skinny brush, and dip it in the tail color to paint short, slanted lines for the top and bottom fins.

Paint the eye and lip

Use your skinny brush with red paint to fill in the middle of the eye. Then make a red line for the mouth. Rinse the brush, and use black paint to paint a pupil in the eye.

Add white lines

Use your skinny brush to make a small fan-shaped fin behind and below the gill line. Also add some lines to the tail, curving them out at the top and bottom to fit the fin shape.

Dot the eye

Last, add a tiny dot of white off center in your fish's eye. For extra decoration, I painted little purple lines between all the fin and tail lines.

Add finishing touches

If you want, you can paint your fish with glitter paint or (if you won't be putting your fish in water) white glue sprinkled with glitter. I also added dots of paint to the body.

13

rocky roadsters

❝ I made a race-track in my sandbox and I needed some cars to put on the roads. My brother said sand would jam up the wheels of toy cars, so I decided to make "rockmobiles" instead. This is how I made them. ❞

What You'll Need

- Rock
- Pencil
- Palette or paper plate
- Paint of your choice
- Paintbrushes
- Black marker (optional)
- Acrylic floor wax (optional)

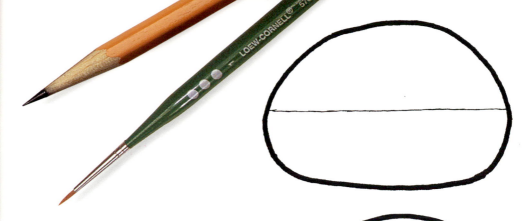

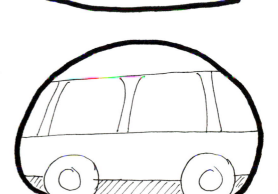

1

Pick a car-shaped rock

Rocks with flat bottoms and rounded tops make good cars. Rocks with square corners can be trucks. You might even find a rock shaped like a roadster with a long hood. Wash your rock and scrub away any slimy stuff.

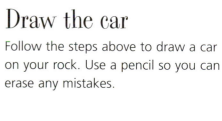

2

Draw the car

Follow the steps above to draw a car on your rock. Use a pencil so you can erase any mistakes.

15

Here's how I drew the car on my rock.

PAINTING TIP

For better results, pull your brush across the rock in smooth strokes instead of dabbing on the paint.

Remember to rinse your brush after each color.

3

Paint the tires

Mix two drops of white with one drop of black to make gray. Use your small brush to fill in all the wheel circles. All four wheels should be the same size and as round as you can make them.

4

Make part of the rock "disappear"

It's almost magical the way painting an area black makes that part of the rock seem to vanish. Use black paint to fill in the space around the bottoms of the wheels and below the car body on both sides and each end.

5

Paint the car body

Pick a color for your car. Dark colors cover in one coat, but a light color may need two coats. Use your medium brush to paint the sides and ends. Then paint the top. Let the paint dry before going to the next step.

Paint the windows

Paint the windows black. Use the skinny brush to paint around the edges, making them as smooth and straight as you can. Then use a bigger brush to fill in the centers.

Paint the wheel hubs

While you still have black paint on your skinny brush, make a big circle in the center of each wheel and fill it in with solid black. Make all these wheel hubs the same size.

Paint the fenders

Use a black marker or your skinny brush with black paint thinned with a little water to paint the curved fenders above each wheel. Connect the front and back fenders with a straight line. Paint two lines for the door (see step 10 for a picture of the door).

Paint the bumpers

Clean your brush. Between the fenders, use white to paint bumpers with rounded corners. Paint a license plate on the back bumper. After the paint dries, use the skinny brush or a marker to paint letters or numbers on the license plate.

10

Paint wheel spokes

Use your skinny brush to paint a white circle inside each black hub circle. Paint an X in the middle, then paint a line sideways and one up and down.

11

Paint the door handles

Then use the same brush to paint white curved lines for the door handles.

12

Paint the steering wheel

Use the same brush to paint a white steering wheel on the driver's side of the front windshield. Paint round white headlights and smaller taillights. Painting white first will make the red and yellow paint show up better.

13

Paint headlights and taillights

When the white is dry, use red paint for the taillights and bright yellow paint for the headlights. You can add sparkle with glitter paint if you want. For a shiny car, paint it with clear acrylic floor wax.

more ideas

rocky roadsters

SCHOOL BUS

19

lazy lizards

" A big green lizard was sunning himself on a rock in our garden. When I tried to catch him, he scurried away, so I took the rock inside and painted my own lizard on it. This lizard never runs away from me! Here is how I did it. "

What You'll Need

Large rock
Pencil
Palette or paper plate
Paint of your choice
Paintbrushes
Dimensional paint (optional)

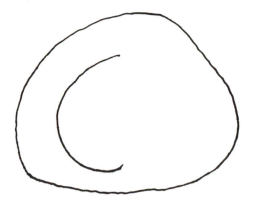
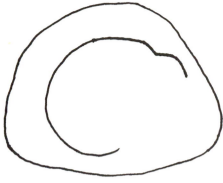

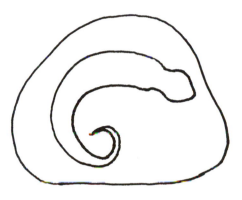

Follow these steps to draw a lizard

1

Choose a rock and draw the lizard

Your rock should be smooth and have enough room in the middle to fit a lizard's curved body and tail. Scrub the rock and draw the lizard on it. Trace this lizard and enlarge it on a copy machine or draw your own lizard following the steps shown above.

Make shadows

Use black paint and your small brush to paint thick black shadows around part of the lizard. Make the shadows below the legs thinner.

Paint the lizard yellow

Rinse your brush and paint the lizard yellow to make the final coat of paint look brighter. Use a small brush to outline the lizard and to fill in the toes and the tip of the tail. Then use a bigger brush to fill in the rest.

Paint the body

I painted my lizard green, but yours can be any color you like. Use your medium brush to paint the top of the lizard's body, leaving an oval-shaped area for the eye. Also leave his tummy and parts of the tail and legs yellow. Use your skinny brush for the toes, tip of the tail and under the eye.

Add stripes

Mix a darker color (I mixed blue and green). Use your small brush to paint a line along the top edge of the yellow tummy, the legs, tail and top of the body.

PAINTING TIP

A long line should be painted in one long, smooth stroke instead of lots of small sketchy lines.

Add rows of spots

Use the same color to make two rows of dots from the neck to the end of the tail, making the dots smaller as you go. Make them big enough so you can paint yellow spots on top.

Fill in the eye

Rinse your brush and use black paint to paint a small oval eye in the center of the yellow eye area. Give the eye pointed ends like a little football. Also make two tiny black dots for nostrils at the end of the nose.

Paint white highlights

Use your small brush to add a line of white along the bottom edge of the lizard to help the yellow tummy stand out. Paint white on the neck, under the chin and around the eye. Make a tiny white dot in the eye.

Add finishing touches

Use a small brush or dimensional paint to paint a yellow dot on the top edge of each blue-green spot so that a little of the darker color shows.

FIXING MISTAKES

If you mess up, wipe off the wet paint with a damp tissue. Then let it dry and try again.

Lizards and salamanders can be painted in a rainbow of colors. Paint a whole collection to decorate your rock garden or fill a terrarium.

flower power

66 My grand-
mother's birthday was
coming, and I wanted
to make something
special for her. She
really likes flowers, so
I thought; "Why not
paint a flower rock
for her?" She loves it!
Here's how I did it. 99

What You'll Need

Large rock

Pencil

White colored pencil

Palette or paper plate

Paint of your choice

Paintbrushes

Clear acrylic spray (optional)

1

Choose a rock

Lots of rock sizes and shapes make good flower rocks. You can use round rocks or chunky rocks that will stand up on one flat end. Whatever the shape, rocks that have mostly smooth surfaces are the easiest to paint. When you have your rock, scrub it and let it dry.

2

Divide your rock

Use a pencil to make a line around the bottom third of your rock. Keep this line as level as possible all the way around or your flower bowl will look uneven.

Remember to rinse your brush

after each color.

3

Paint the bowl

Pick a color for the bowl. I chose blue to match my grandmother's sofa. Add two drops of white to this color. Use your biggest brush to paint the bowl all the way down to the bottom. Let the paint dry.

Paint the background

Rinse your brush and mix green with enough black to make a very dark green. A dark color behind the leaves and flowers will make them stand out. Paint this color from the top down to the bowl. Let the paint dry.

Draw the leaves

Use a white pencil to draw different-size oval leaves. Start with a cluster at the top, then work down. Overlap the leaves and draw a few that hang over the edge of the bowl. It's OK to have irregular spaces between the leaves.

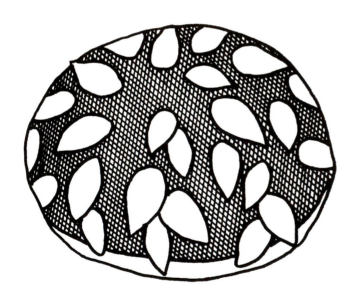

Your leaves should look something like this.

Paint some of the leaves

Use a small or medium brush and green paint to paint all the leaves at the very top of your rock. Then use this same color to paint other leaves here and there.

7 Paint light green leaves

Rinse your brush and mix equal amounts of yellow and green to make light green. Use this to paint more leaves, again skipping around.

8 Paint the rest of the leaves

Finally, add a little more green to the light green mixture to make an in-between color and paint the rest of the leaves.

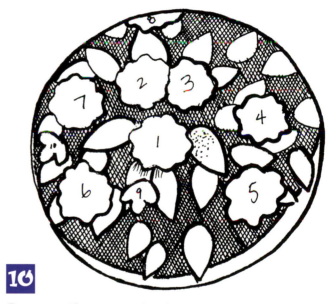

9 Detail the leaves

Mix a little black with green to make dark green. Use a skinny brush to add a crease down the center of all the dark green leaves. Use plain green to paint the creases in the other leaves. Use black paint to outline the places where the leaves overlap.

10 Draw flower shapes

When the paint is dry, use a white pencil to draw three flowers in the center (numbers 1, 2 and 3 above). Add others around the edges (4 to 8). Numbers 9 and 10 are buds. Draw some flowers close together and others farther apart.

Paint white flowers

Use your medium brush and white paint to fill in all the flower shapes. Let it dry and paint a second coat if needed.

Add petal details

An easy way to paint flowers is to paint a curl in the middle of each flower with a small brush and red paint. Begin in the center each time. The spirals will look better if they are a little uneven or if there are small gaps in the lines.

Add flower buds

Fill in any plain-looking places with a few flower buds. Mix pale pink by adding a touch of red to a drop of white. Use your medium brush to make a center oval shape and add two smaller ovals, one on each side.

Paint bud details

Use your small brush with red paint to outline the inside edges of the two side ovals, and one straight line up the center. Rinse the brush and use the dark green from step 9 to paint a cluster of lines on the top of the bud.

flower power

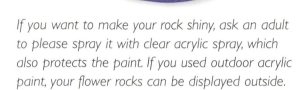

There are lots of
ways to paint flowers
on rocks.

If you want to make your rock shiny, ask an adult
to please spray it with clear acrylic spray, which
also protects the paint. If you used outdoor acrylic
paint, your flower rocks can be displayed outside.

You can paint
flowers on a rock
that is too uneven
to stand on its
own. "Plant" it in
a flowerpot!

rockosaurs

" What would it be like to have a dinosaur for a pet? I guess I'd need a bigger room! I painted some dinosaurs on rocks and took them to school when we were studying prehistoric reptiles. Everyone thought they were cool. "

What You'll Need

Large rock

Pencil

Palette or paper plate

Paint of your choice

Paintbrushes

Cotton swab (optional)

Black marker (optional)

Paint a basecoat

A coat of yellow paint will make the final paint color look brighter, especially on dark-colored rocks. Use your large brush to paint the whole rock, except for the very bottom. Let the paint dry before you go on. Clean your brush.

Choose a rock

Rocks with flat bottoms and curving tops work best. Scrub your rock clean. If the bottom of your rock is not level, add air-dry clay to the wet rock as shown on page 45. Let the clay dry overnight before painting your rock.

Paint the rock orange

Paint the rock orange, which is red mixed with yellow, or choose another color. Let it dry.

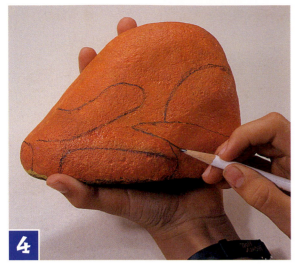

On the front of your rock, draw an oval about the size of your thumbprint. Add neck lines to the head, curving them down and around the corner of the rock but leaving room below the bottom neck line for the front legs.

4

Draw the dinosaur

Follow the drawings to draw a dinosaur on your rock.

Draw the tail so the tip points to the neck. Draw the front leg, then a tummy line from behind the front leg to the tail.

Make a big oval haunch that curves above the top of the tail. Draw a back foot where the tail curves up from the bottom of the rock.

Turn your rock around and draw the other front leg. Draw another oval haunch and back leg plus a tummy line between the two legs.

Here is the way your rock should look from the front edge.

Paint the open spaces

Use a medium or large brush with black paint to darken the spaces around the legs and below the body.

Paint black on the back

Also darken the spaces between the two front legs and around the legs on the back of the rock.

Add shading

Add enough water to some brown paint so you can see through it. Use a cotton swab or paintbrush to add brown shadows below the head and neck, around the haunch and under the tail. Before the paint dries, soften the edges of the shadows by rubbing them with a dry paintbrush.

Add shading to the back

Add shadows to the back of your dinosaur around the haunch and on the bottom of the tummy.

Paint highlights

Mix two drops of yellow with one drop of white. Use a damp cotton swab or medium stiff brush to scrub this color along the top half of the head and neck, the top of the haunch and the top of the tail. Soften the edges with a dry paintbrush.

Repeat

Paint highlights along the top edge of the haunch on the back side, too.

11 Add spots

Use the same cotton swab (or a small brush) and yellow paint to add clusters of spots to the top of the dinosaur.

12 Add black details

Use your small brush and black paint (or a black marker) to make a tiny dot for a nostril, a curved mouth line and a round eye. Then outline the head, neck, haunches and tail with black paint to make them stand out.

13 Add yellow details

Rinse your brush and make light outlines along the tummy, the tail and the neck with the yellow paint from step 9. Add a row of short, curved lines to the bottom edge of the tail and longer curved lines on the tummy. Turn the rock over and paint tummy lines on the back of the dinosaur.

14 Add white touches

Use your small brush and white paint to make a tiny C shape inside the black eye circle. If you mess up, let the paint dry, then fix it with black paint. Paint a white dot in the eye. Add three half-circle toenails to each foot.

15 Create more texture

Pick up a little red paint with a clean, damp cotton swab or your small brush to add more dots to the dinosaur's back and the tops of the haunches. Add smaller dots to the yellow places on the neck and tail.

Look at your rock from every angle to make sure it looks finished.

more ideas

There are lots of other kinds of dinosaurs that you can paint on rocks. You could even try turning a dinosaur into a dragon!

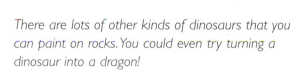

6

go buggy!

"When I told my friends I was going to give them cooties, you should have seen the faces they made! Now everyone wants me to "bug" them! Here is how I painted my cootie bugs."

What You'll Need

Rock
White colored pencil
Palette or paper plate
Paint of your choice
Paintbrushes
Black marker (optional)
Glitter paint (optional)

1 Pick a rock

Any size smooth, round or oval rock will work, but tiny rocks may be harder to paint. Scrub it clean.

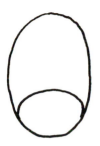

2 Paint a basecoat

Use a big flat brush to paint the top and sides of your rock with a light color of paint. You can leave the bottom unpainted. Let the paint dry.

3 Sketch the design

Use a white pencil to draw the bug. Make a line for the head, and add three curved lines for stripes. You may use a regular pencil, but draw the lines lightly so they won't show through the paint.

4

Paint the head and one stripe

Pick a different color and use your large brush to paint the head, making the edges neat and round. Then paint the third stripe this color.

5

Paint another stripe

Rinse your brush. When the paint is dry, paint the second stripe with bright red or a different color of your choice.

6

Paint the last stripe

Rinse your brush, then choose another color to paint the back end of the bug, covering the basecoat to the very bottom edges of the rock. I used a mixture of yellow and green.

7

Draw and paint the eyes

To keep the eyes level, sketch a straight line across the top part of the head and draw two round eyes that are the same size. Use your small brush and white paint to fill in the eye circles.

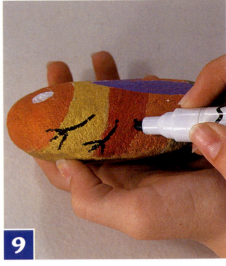

Draw and paint the wings

When the stripes are dry, draw two long oval wings that come to points at the center of the first stripe. Use a large or medium brush and a new color of paint to fill in these wing shapes. I used purple.

Add legs and feet

Use your small brush and black paint (or a black marker) to draw three curved legs on each side of its body. Draw the feet any shape you wish.

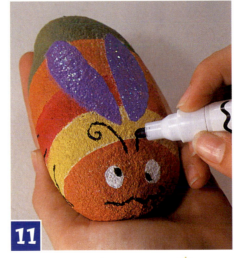
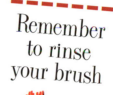

Remember to rinse your brush

after each color.

Add glitter if you want

I added glitter paint to the wings, but you may want to put glitter on one of the stripes instead. Use your imagination to make your bug special.

Add details

Use a black marker or a small brush and black paint to give your bug a wiggly mouth line, two goofy-looking eyeballs and a pair of curly feelers.

more ideas

There are lots of different bugs you can paint, from ones that look real to some that are really silly.

sandbox city

"My rock cars gave me the idea to make a city to go with them. I looked around and found lots of rocks shaped like all kinds of buildings. They were fun to paint, too. Here's how you can make a really easy rock house."

What You'll Need ↪

Rock

Pencil

Palette or paper plate

Paint of your choice

Paintbrushes

Cotton swab (optional)

Black marker (optional)

1

Pick a rock

Rocks for buildings should have flat bottoms and flat fronts. Rocks with square tops make good stores. Houses should have slanted or pointed tops. Scrub the rock clean.

2

Draw the design

Use a pencil to sketch the door in the center of the rock. Draw square or rectangular windows on each side of the door so that the tops line up. Make a third window near the top. Draw two straight lines along the front, sides and the back for the roof. If your rock is thick enough, add windows to the sides of the rock.

3

Paint the walls

Your house may be any color you like. I mixed black and white to make gray. Use a large or medium brush to paint the front, sides and back of your house, leaving the doors, windows and roof unpainted.

4

Paint the roof

Rinse your brush and paint the roof but not the area under it, which is called the eaves. I painted my roof black. Other good color combinations are white walls with a dark green roof, light blue walls with a navy blue roof, yellow walls with a brown roof, and red walls with a white roof.

5

Paint the windows

Yellow windows make your house look cheerful and cozy. If your walls are yellow, paint the windows orange or a dark color. Use your small brush, and make the edges of the windows as straight as you can.

6

Add a glow

Mix a tiny amount of orange (red plus yellow). Use the tip of your finger, a damp cotton swab or a small, dry brush to rub this color on the bottom part of each window.

7

Paint the door and eaves

Use a small or medium brush and white paint to neatly fill in the shape of the door, keeping the edges smooth and straight. If there is room, add a doorstep below the door. Paint a white line under the roof for the eaves.

8

Add black outlines

Use black paint and the skinny brush or a black marker to outline the door, the doorstep and the windows. Make a cross in each window. Straight lines in the corners help make the house look square. Add a doorknob.

9

Paint some bushes

Rinse your brush and mix green with a small amount of black to make dark green. Use this paint and your small brush to make pointed oval bushes on each side of the door and at the two corners of the house.

10

Paint flowers

Rinse your brush and switch to plain green to paint flower stems under each window. Keep them shorter than the bushes. Let these lines dry and rinse your brush before adding red flowers to the tops and middles of the stems.

Paint flowers on the bushes

Use the very tip of your skinniest brush to add dots for tiny flowers all over the bushes. I used purple. Now your rock house is finished!

11

more ideas

There are lots of other kinds of rock buildings you can paint to add to your sandbox city. Look at the buildings in your neighborhood for ideas.

TOY STORE

GAS STATION

SWEET SHOP

OPEN

how to fix a wobbly rock!

What do you do with a rock that won't stand up? Add some air-dry clay to the bottom. The place where the clay was added won't show once the rock has been painted. This air-dry clay is sold at craft stores, but you can use any kind of clay that hardens without baking.

1 Scrub the rock clean. Clay sticks best to a wet rock.

2 Put clay on the bottom of the rock and smooth it with your fingers. There shouldn't be any bumps where the clay and the rock meet.

3 Stand the rock on a table so the bottom of the clay becomes flat. If the rock still tips over, add more clay until the rock stands up. Leave the rock alone for 24 hours until the clay is dry.

playful food

66 Did you ever pretend to run a restaurant? You can paint rocks to look like lots of different kinds of food. I made hamburgers for my picnic table restaurant. My dad thought they looked so good that he bought one to use as a paperweight on his desk. Here's how I made them. 99

What You'll Need

Rock

Pencil

White colored pencil

Palette or paper plate

Paint of your choice

Paintbrushes

White dimensional paint (optional)

2

Draw the bun lines

Draw a line all around the rock, a little bit above the center. Make another line below the first line, leaving enough space for the burger patty and toppings.

1

Find a hamburger-shaped rock

Look for round rocks that are flat on the bottom and rounded on top. They can be as big or small as you wish, but a rock that fits into your hand is perfect. Scrub the rock clean and let it dry.

3

Paint the meat

Use your large or medium brush and brown paint to paint the meat, keeping the top and bottom edges as smooth and level as you can. Let the paint dry.

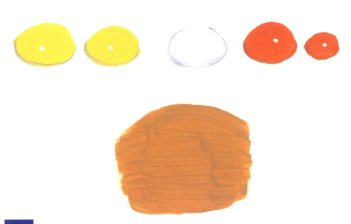

4

Mix paint for the bun

Use your large brush to mix two drops of yellow, one drop of white, and one and a half drops of orange. Put a small drop of brown on your palette and pick up a little on the tip of your brush. Add it to the mix. Add touches of brown and white until the mixture is the color of a bun.

5

Paint the bun

Use your large brush to cover the entire top half of the bun with the bun color. When you are finished, don't rinse your brush, but use it to mix the next color.

Prop up your rock with a brush or a pencil when you paint the bottom bun. Let the paint dry before going on.

6

Paint a tan ring and the bottom bun

The bun should be lighter just above the meat. Mix a drop or two of white paint with the paint left on your brush to make tan. Paint a narrow ring just above the meat. Use a dry brush to soften the edge where the two colors meet. Paint the bottom bun this tan color, too.

Remember to rinse your brush

after each color.

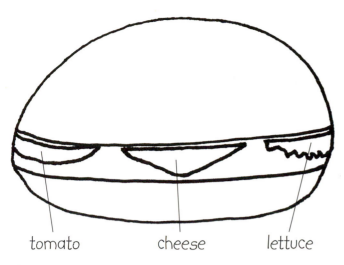

tomato   cheese   lettuce

7

Add the fillings

Use a white pencil to sketch four cheese triangles equally spaced around your meat. In the upper half of the meat, sketch a half-round tomato slice between the first two triangles, a ruffled edge of lettuce leaf between the next two, then another tomato slice and a final lettuce leaf.

8

Paint a basecoat for the fillings

To help the fillings stand out, use your medium brush with yellow to paint all the shapes you just sketched. Leave a narrow ring of brown paint showing along the tops of the fillings. Make sure the edge of the lettuce looks wavy.

9

Paint the cheese and tomato

Rinse your brush. Then mix a tiny amount of red into a small drop of yellow to make a cheese color. Paint all four cheese triangles with this color. Rinse your brush and use red paint to paint the two tomato slices.

Paint the lettuce

10

Rinse your brush. Squeeze out a drop of yellow paint and add a little white and green to make a pale green color. Paint the two lettuce leaves, leaving a line of brown just above them.

Detail the lettuce

11

Add more green to the lettuce color and use this darker shade to paint short lines on the lettuce so it looks ruffled.

Dot the top of the bun

12

Use your smallest brush and brown paint to paint small dark dots over the top of the bun. (I made about fifty!) Don't put any around the sides.

Add sesame seeds

13

You can paint the seeds with white paint, or you can make real-looking seeds with white dimensional paint. Touch the tip of the bottle just off center of each brown spot, then lift up sideways. A rim of brown should show on one side. If you mess up, use a damp cotton swab to pick up the paint. When all the seeds are painted, let it dry for an hour.

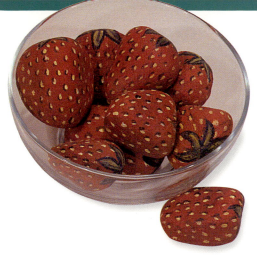

more ideas

Try painting some pickle chips and sliced tomatoes to serve with your "burgers."

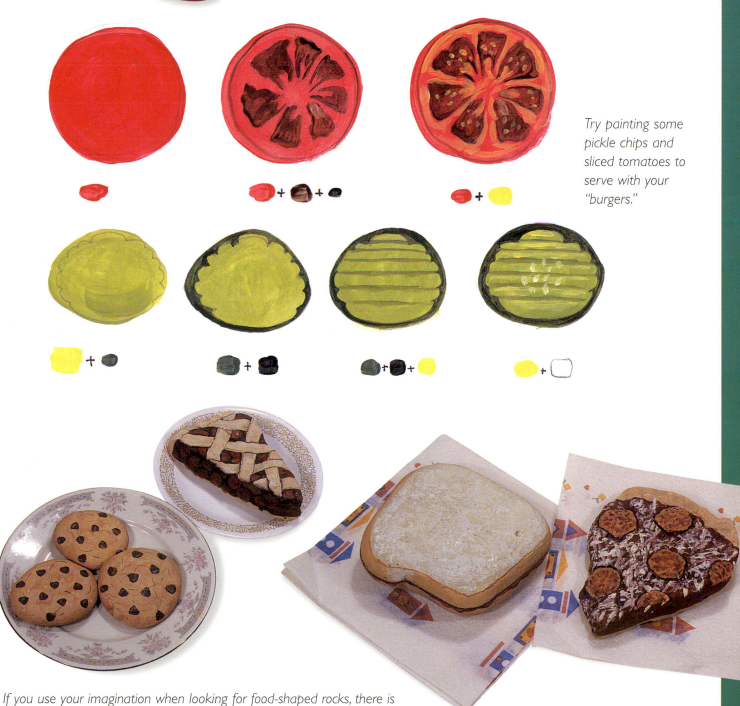

If you use your imagination when looking for food-shaped rocks, there is no telling what you'll find: sandwiches, cookies, fruit, or slices of pie or pizza, to name just a few!

mystery eggs

66 What if you discovered a strange-looking egg just as it was starting to hatch? What kind of creature would be inside? A dragon? A dinosaur? An alien? Maybe even a monster? Paint one and maybe you'll find out! 99

What You'll Need ↴

- Large rock
- Pencil
- White colored pencil (optional)
- Palette or paper plate
- Paint of your choice
- Paintbrushes
- Sponge
- Silver acrylic paint (optional)
- Glow-in-the-dark paint (optional)
- Black marker (optional)

1

Choose an egg-shaped rock

Any of these rocks would make a good egg. Look for an oval rock that is shaped like an egg. It can be any size, but one that is about as big as your fist makes a good first egg. Scrub it clean and let it dry.

2

Paint the basecoat

Use your large brush to mix two big drops of white with one big drop of black. Paint your entire rock with this gray color. Let it dry before going to the next step.

3

Tear a sponge

Tear a small piece from a kitchen sponge so that it has ragged edges. Wet it and squeeze most of the water out.

4

Sponge on purple paint

Use a brush to spread a small puddle of purple paint (red mixed with blue) on your palette. Lightly press the damp sponge piece into the paint. Dab the sponge on a piece of newspaper, then pat it on your painted rock, turning it in different directions. You may have to do this several times. Let the paint dry.

5

Sponge on blue paint

Pour out a small puddle of blue paint. Rinse your sponge and squeeze it almost dry. Sponge blue paint on your rock just as you did in step 4. Let the paint dry. Rinse your sponge clean.

6

Sponge on silver paint

Now sponge on a coat of silver acrylic paint. If you don't have silver paint, use light gray. Sponge this color lightly so that the other colors show through. Let the paint dry.

7 ## Outline the opening

Sketch a diamond-shaped opening on your rock, using the drawing at left as a guide. Use your small brush and black paint to outline the shape of the jagged hole. Wiggle your brush as you paint to make wavy lines.

8 Paint the center

Switch to your large brush to fill in the center of the shape with solid black.

9 Create large cracks

Use your smallest brush and black paint to paint large cracks around the outside of the opening. Make some thick and some thin, some short and some longer so that they don't look too much alike.

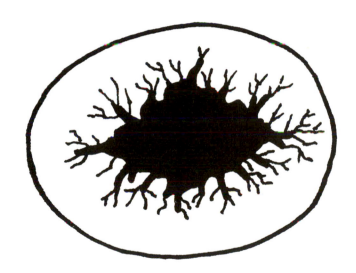

Remember
to rinse
your brush

after
each color.

10 Make tiny cracks

To make the smaller cracks, you can use a fine-tip black marker or a paint pen. Or mix a little water with some black paint and use the tip of your small brush to paint thin crooked lines that fan out from the ends of the cracks, some with two lines, some with more.

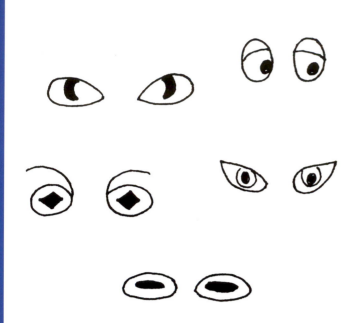

11

Paint the eyes

When the black paint is dry, use your small brush and white paint to paint two small eyes that are the same size. The eyes can be any shape you like. It may help to sketch them first with a white pencil. Let the paint dry.

12

Paint the eye color

Mix lime green from yellow with just a touch of blue, or use glow-in-the-dark paint for a spooky effect. Use your small brush to paint this color over the white eye shapes.

13

Paint the pupils

Clean your small brush, then use black paint or a black marker to add two pupils. I made mine narrow and curved like cats' eyes. The pupils you paint may be different.

mystery eggs

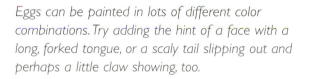

Eggs can be painted in lots of different color combinations. Try adding the hint of a face with a long, forked tongue, or a scaly tail slipping out and perhaps a little claw showing, too.

bookend bears

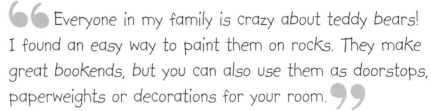

> Everyone in my family is crazy about teddy bears! I found an easy way to paint them on rocks. They make great bookends, but you can also use them as doorstops, paperweights or decorations for your room.

Large rock

Pencil

Palette or paper plate

Paint of your choice

Paintbrushes

Cotton swab (optional)

Marker (optional)

1

Find a bear-shaped rock

Look for tall rocks with flat bottoms. They can have a slight tilt to them. Medium-size ones are easiest to paint. Scrub the rock clean. If your rock won't stand up, add air-dry clay to the bottom as shown on page 45. Let the clay dry overnight before painting your rock.

2

Paint your rock

Use your large brush to paint the entire rock the color you've chosen for your bear. If your rock is dark, you may need to add a second coat. Let the paint dry.

3

Sketch the bear

Use a pencil to draw the bear on your rock, following the drawings on the next page.

59

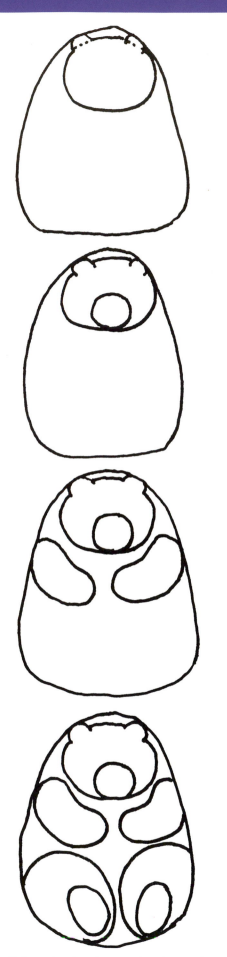

Follow the drawings to sketch your bear.

4

Paint dark outlines

Use dark paint and a small brush or a marker to paint over the pencil lines. Use brown paint if your bear is yellow or tan. If your bear is a different color, use a darker shade of the body color.

5

Paint fuzzy shadows

Dabbing in shadows with a brush or cotton swab will make your bear look fuzzy. Dip your small brush or swab in the dark paint from step 4 and dab it on newspaper first. Then dab the paint in the middle of the tummy and around the arms, legs and the head.

6

Paint the back

Turn the rock over and dab soft shadows at the bottom. Dab wing-shaped shoulder blades just above the center. Also add some shadows behind the ears.

7

Add fuzzy highlights

Mix a tiny dot of your bear's main color with a drop of white paint. Use a clean, damp cotton swab or paintbrush to dot this color around the ears, the top of the head, the tops of the arms and the tops of the legs.

8

Paint the muzzle and feet

Use a small or medium brush and plain white paint to paint the muzzle and the bottoms of the feet.

9

Add black touches

Use your small brush and black paint to darken the shadows around the bottom edge of the head, the bottom edges of the front feet and between the legs. Then paint two small eyes, a small round nose and two curved mouth lines below the nose.

Paint the toes

Use black paint to add three small toe lines to each foot. If you like your bear, go to step 13, or you can follow the next steps to add furry details.

Add fur (optional)

To make your bear look furry, add a little water to the color you used in step 7. Use your smallest brush to add tiny lines around the head, ears, legs, and the tops and bottoms of the arms. Add these lines to the shadows on the back of the bear, too.

Add furry shadows (optional)

Rinse your brush and add a little water to the dark color you used in step 4. Make clusters of short brown lines on the bear's cheeks. Also add a row of lines along the bottoms of the arms and legs.

Paint eye highlight

A tiny dot of pure white off center in each black eye will make your bear seem to be looking back at you!

bookend bears

Tiny bears make great gifts or party favors. Doll-size straw hats from a craft store come in different sizes to fit almost any rock bear.

more fun books for creative kids!

Try these fun, no-mess projects inspired by your favorite stories, including *How Many Bugs in a Box*, *I Wish I Were a Butterfly*, *Gingerbread Baby* and more. You'll learn how to make soft felt boxes, lace-wing butterfly barrettes, a milk carton gingerbread house and other exciting creations. There are 26 projects in each volume!

Volume 1: ISBN 1-58180-059-2, paperback, 128 pages, #31622-K

Volume 2: ISBN 1-58180-088-6, paperback, 128 pages, #31688-K

This book is packed with all sorts of art adventures that help you get creative and have tons of fun! You'll learn how to draw, paint, sculpt in clay, create life-size portraits, and make incredible prints with soap blocks, buttons, leaves, and more.

ISBN 0-89134-833-6, paperback, 216 pages, #30973-K

If you like to creating your own easy, exciting fun-filled craft projects, you'll love this book. It will show you how to make costumes, clothes—even gifts for friends and family. You'll also find plenty of crazy crafts like puppets, checkerboards, plus other toys and games.

ISBN 0-89134-834-4, paperback, 216 pages, #30974-K

Oh, the things you can create with paper! Learn how to make paper stars, party streamers, lanterns, hanging baskets, paper beads, handmade books, decoupage and more. These crafts are perfect for parties, rainy days and gift giving, plus they're easy to do and fun to make.

ISBN 1-58180-290-0, paperback, 64 pages, #32167-K

These and other Creative Kids titles are available at your favorite arts & crafts store, bookstore or library. You or your parents can call 1-800-289-0963 for more information!